The AI Revolution:
Are You Ready?

By
Berkay Avci

Copyright © 2024

All rights reserved.

No part of this book may be used or reproduced by any means, graphic, electronic, or mechanical, including photocopying, recording, taping, or by any information storage retrieval system, without the written permission of the publisher except in the case of brief quotations embodied in critical articles and reviews.

Foreword

A Symphony of Human and Machine We all dream of a future brimming with possibility, a world where technology amplifies our potential and ignites solutions to the challenges we face. Artificial intelligence (AI) stands poised to usher in this new era, but the key lies not just in the algorithms and circuits, but in the spark of human ingenuity. This book is an invitation to join the orchestra of innovation. It's a call to those who dare to dream, who see the world not for what it is, but for what it could become. Whether you're an artist yearning to express yourself in new ways, a social entrepreneur seeking to bridge divides, or simply someone with a nagging question about the world, this book will equip you with the tools to turn your vision into reality.

Here's the beauty: you don't need to be a tech whiz to be a part of this revolution. This book speaks to the artist in all of us, the one who sees connections where others see walls, who can translate a problem into a symphony of human and machine working in concert. The pages that follow hold the potential to ignite a fire within you. They offer not just knowledge, but inspiration, a call to unleash the creativity that resides within each of us. It's a chance to be a part of something bigger, to leave a mark on the world, and to build a future brimming with wonder and possibility. So, turn the page, my friend. Let the music begin.

Table of Contents

Introduction: Welcome to the Age of Intelligent Machines. 1

Chapter 1: Welcome to the AI Age 2
    A Brief History of AI: From Dream to Reality 2
    The Many Faces of AI: A Spectrum of Intelligence 3
    Why Now? The Perfect Storm for the AI Revolution 4

Chapter 2: AI in Action: Transforming Our World (Part 1) - Healthcare: From Superhuman Doctors to Chatbots (Not the Chatty Kind from Your Dating App) 5

Chapter 2: AI in Action: Transforming Our World (Part 2) - From Shopping Sprees to Self-Driving Cars: AI is Everywhere (Except Maybe Your Refrigerator... Yet) 7
    Retail: From Impulse Buys to Personalized Recommendations 7
    Finance: From Risky Investments to Robo-Advisors 8
    Transportation: Buckle Up for Self-Driving Cars (Maybe Not Quite Yet) 8

Chapter 2: AI in Action: Transforming Our World (Part 3) - From Smarter Schools to Spooky Security Systems: AI is Everywhere (Except Maybe Your Refrigerator... Still) 10
    Education: From Textbooks to Personalized Learning 10
    Manufacturing: From Assembly Lines to Smart Factories 11
    Security: From Guard Dogs to AI-powered Surveillance .. 11

Chapter 2: AI in Action: Transforming Our World (Part 4) - A Peek into the AI-Powered Future: From Leisure to Agriculture (and Maybe Even Your Refrigerator, Eventually) 12

Entertainment: From Binge-Watching to Personalized Playlists on Autopilot 12

Agriculture: From Backbreaking Labor to Smart Farming Revolution 13

The Future of AI: From Your Smartphone to Your Refrigerator (Eventually) 13

Chapter 3: The Road Ahead: Opportunities and Challenges of the AI Revolution 15

Part 1: A World of Opportunity 15

Part 2: Challenges and Ethical Considerations 16

Conclusion: Shaping the Future of AI 17

Chapter 4: You and the AI Revolution: Are You Ready?. 18

Developing Your AI Literacy 18

Cultivating Essential Skills for the AI Era 19

Leveraging AI in Your Daily Life 21

Conclusion 22

    Embrace the Power of "Both/And," Not "Either/Or" ... 23

    Become an Advocate for Responsible AI 23

    Be a Force for Positive Change 23

    The Future is Yours to Shape 24

    Call to Action: Your AI Adventure Continues 24

Chapter 5: Unleashing the Power of AI: Your Gateway to Passive Income! 27

From Etsy Shop to AI Powerhouse: The Story of Sarah and Her Personalized Jewelry Line 27

From Struggling Musician to AI-powered Composer: The Rise of David 27

Get Ready to Be Amazed: A Sneak Peek into the Future of AI and Passive Income 28

Why AI Makes Passive Income Your Superpower 29
20 AI-Powered Business Ideas for Passive Income (Even with No Money!) 30
    Free or Low-Cost Ideas: 31
    Ideas Requiring Some Investment: 32
    1. AI-powered Content Creation Assistant: Your Secret Weapon for Effortless Content 34
    2. Virtual Assistant with an AI Edge: Automate Tasks, Boost Productivity 36
    3. AI-Powered Social Media Management: Effortless Engagement for Busy Businesses 41
Launching Your AI-Powered Business: From Idea to Action 47
    1. Refine Your Business Idea: 47
    2. Develop a Minimum Viable Product (MVP): 48
    3. Build Your Brand Identity: 48
    4. Marketing and Customer Acquisition: 49
    5. Legal and Financial Considerations: 49

Chapter 6: Unleash Your Inner AI Entrepreneur: Fueling Motivation and Inspiration 51
    Spark Your Creativity: Reimagine the Future with AI 51
    Fueling Your Passion: Inspiration from AI Trailblazers 51
    Beyond Inspiration: Practical Steps to Get Started 52
    Bonus Tip: Leverage the Power of ChatGPT 52
    Building Your AI Business Vocabulary 53
        Dictionary of Modern AI Terms 53

Introduction: Welcome to the Age of Intelligent Machines

The world is on the cusp of a revolution. Artificial intelligence (AI) is rapidly transforming every aspect of our lives, from the way we work and shop to how we receive medical care and navigate our cities. It's no longer science fiction; AI is here, and its impact is undeniable.

But are you ready?

This book, The AI Revolution: Are You Ready?, is your guide to understanding the exciting potential and profound challenges of this technological leap. We'll delve into the fascinating world of AI, exploring its history, different forms, and the remarkable applications already reshaping our reality.

We'll then shift our focus to you, the reader. How will AI impact your career? Can you leverage its power to enhance your daily life? We'll address these questions and many more, equipping you with the knowledge and tools needed to navigate the AI revolution.

Whether you're a business professional, a curious individual, or simply someone concerned about the future, this book is for you. We'll explore not only the "what" and "how" of AI, but also the "why." We'll discuss the ethical considerations surrounding AI development and the steps we can take to ensure it benefits all of humanity

Chapter 1:
Welcome to the AI Age

Welcome to the age of intelligent machines! Imagine a world where machines can diagnose diseases, write realistic news articles, or even hold conversations that feel eerily human. This isn't science fiction anymore; it's the reality we're living in, thanks to the remarkable advancements in Artificial Intelligence (AI).

But what exactly is AI? In its simplest form, AI refers to the ability of machines to exhibit intelligent behavior. This can range from performing tasks that typically require human intelligence, like playing chess or recognizing faces, to even learning and adapting on their own.

The concept of AI has captivated humanity for centuries. Early philosophers pondered the possibility of creating intelligent machines, and science fiction has long explored the potential (and sometimes perils) of AI. However, it's only in recent decades, with the explosion of computing power and data availability, that AI has truly begun to flourish.

A Brief History of AI: From Dream to Reality

The history of AI is a fascinating journey filled with both breakthroughs and setbacks. Here are some key milestones:

- **1950s:** The term "Artificial Intelligence" is coined by John McCarthy at the Dartmouth workshop, marking the formal birth of AI research.
- **1960s:** Early successes in AI include game-playing programs like checkers and chess champions. However, limitations in computing power lead to an "AI Winter" in the following decade.

- **1980s-1990s:** Expert systems gain traction in specific domains, but limitations in knowledge representation hinder broader applications.
- **2000s:** The rise of machine learning, particularly deep learning, marks a turning point. AI algorithms fueled by vast datasets achieve breakthroughs in areas like image recognition and natural language processing.
- **2010s-Present:** AI continues its rapid evolution, with applications permeating every aspect of our lives. From self-driving cars to personalized recommendations, AI is transforming industries and reshaping our world.

The Many Faces of AI: A Spectrum of Intelligence

AI isn't a monolithic entity; it encompasses a wide range of technologies and approaches. Let's explore some of the most common types:

- **Machine Learning:** This type of AI allows algorithms to learn from data without explicit programming. By analyzing vast amounts of data, the algorithms can identify patterns and improve their performance over time.
- **Deep Learning:** A subset of machine learning inspired by the structure and function of the human brain. Deep learning algorithms use artificial neural networks to process information and achieve remarkable results in areas like image and speech recognition.
- **Natural Language Processing (NLP):** This field focuses on enabling computers to understand and process human language. NLP applications include machine translation, chatbots, and sentiment analysis.
- **Computer Vision:** Equips machines with the ability to "see" and interpret the visual world. It is used in

applications like facial recognition, self-driving cars, and medical image analysis.

This is just a glimpse into the diverse landscape of AI. As research continues, we can expect even more sophisticated and groundbreaking forms of artificial intelligence to emerge.

Why Now? The Perfect Storm for the AI Revolution

Several factors have converged to create the perfect storm for the current AI revolution:

- **Exponential Growth in Computing Power:** The ever-increasing power and affordability of computer chips provide the necessary processing muscle for complex AI algorithms.
- **The Data Deluge:** The explosion of digital data generated daily – from social media posts to sensor readings – fuels AI by providing the raw material for learning and improvement.
- **Advancements in Algorithms:** Researchers are constantly developing new and more effective AI algorithms, unlocking capabilities that were previously unimaginable.

These factors, combined with a growing understanding of AI principles, have propelled us into a new era where intelligent machines are no longer a futuristic vision but a tangible reality.

In the next section, we'll delve deeper into the remarkable ways AI is transforming our world. Get ready to be amazed!

Chapter 2:
AI in Action: Transforming Our World (Part 1) - Healthcare: From Superhuman Doctors to Chatbots (Not the Chatty Kind from Your Dating App)

Remember that time you Googled your weird rash and ended up convinced you had a rare, exotic disease (turns out it was just a reaction to your new laundry detergent)? Well, AI in healthcare is here to (hopefully) prevent those late-night internet diagnoses.

Think of AI as your friendly neighborhood superhero in a lab coat. It can:

- **Become a diagnosis ninja:** Forget squinting at X-rays all day. AI algorithms can analyze medical images with superhuman vision, spotting hidden clues to diseases like cancer and heart trouble faster than a speeding bullet (well, maybe not that fast, but definitely faster than you searching WebMD).
- **Predict your medical future:** Just like that creepy fortune teller at the carnival (but hopefully more accurate), AI can analyze your medical history, DNA, and lifestyle habits to identify if you're at risk for certain conditions. This allows doctors to take preventative measures, keeping you healthy and happy (and avoiding those awkward carnival fortune teller predictions).
- **Craft personalized medicine plans:** Imagine a world where your doctor doesn't just prescribe the same medication to everyone. AI can personalize treatment plans based on your unique biology, making them more effective and reducing the risk of nasty side effects. Think of it as a custom-made medicine cocktail, just for you (minus the tiny umbrellas, hopefully).

- **Become your virtual health buddy:** Tired of forgetting to take your meds? Enter the friendly (and hopefully not creepy) AI-powered virtual assistant. It can remind you to take your pills, track your symptoms, and even answer basic health questions you might be too embarrassed to ask your doctor (like why that weird sound keeps coming from your stomach... seriously, though, ask a doctor about that).
- **Take the grunt work out of healthcare:** Imagine a world where chatbots handle appointment scheduling and insurance questions, freeing up doctors and nurses to focus on what they do best: taking care of you! Think of it as having a super-efficient receptionist that never takes a coffee break (although, how fun are those coffee break chats with the receptionist?).

These are just a few ways AI is revolutionizing healthcare. It's not about replacing doctors (although, maybe they'll finally have time to figure out what that sound in your stomach is), but rather about making healthcare more efficient, accurate, and personalized. Stay tuned for the next part, where we'll see how AI is transforming other industries, from finance to retail (and hopefully not turning those chatty dating app bots into our financial advisors... yikes!).

Chapter 2: AI in Action: Transforming Our World (Part 2) - From Shopping Sprees to Self-Driving Cars: AI is Everywhere (Except Maybe Your Refrigerator... Yet)

We left off with the amazing ways AI is revamping healthcare. But buckle up, because this revolution is spreading faster than a social media trend (remember that weird cinnamon challenge? Yeah, AI probably wouldn't recommend that). Here's a glimpse of how AI is transforming other sectors:

Retail: From Impulse Buys to Personalized Recommendations

Remember that time you spent hours browsing online, only to end up with a shopping cart full of things you don't actually need? AI can be your guardian angel (with a credit card limit, hopefully). Here's how:

- **Recommending things you'll actually use:** AI algorithms can analyze your past purchases and browsing habits to suggest products you might genuinely like, unlike your friend who keeps recommending that weird juicer you'll never use.
- **Predicting what you'll want before you even know it:** Ever feel like stores can read your mind? Well, with AI, they kind of can. By analyzing trends and customer behavior, AI can predict what products will be popular, ensuring stores have what you need before you even realize you need it (dangerous for your wallet, but convenient nonetheless).

Finance: From Risky Investments to Robo-Advisors

Investing can feel like navigating a financial jungle gym. But fear not, AI is here to be your not-so-distant cousin who aced finance class (and hopefully isn't secretly plotting to steal your inheritance). Here's how AI is changing the game:

- **Spotting risky investments:** AI algorithms can analyze vast amounts of financial data to identify potential risks in investments, helping you avoid putting your hard-earned money into a house of cards.
- **Robo-advisors to the rescue!:** Don't have the time or expertise to manage your own investments? Enter the robo-advisor, an AI-powered tool that can create personalized investment plans based on your risk tolerance and financial goals. Think of it as a financial advisor who works 24/7 and never needs a coffee break (although, sometimes a human touch is still important).

Transportation: Buckle Up for Self-Driving Cars (Maybe Not Quite Yet)

Remember those futuristic movies with self-driving cars? Well, the future is kind of here, with AI playing a big role in transforming transportation. Get ready for:

- **Self-driving cars (eventually):** AI-powered autonomous vehicles promise a future with safer, more efficient roads. Imagine cruising down the highway while catching up on emails or (safely!) watching a movie (although, maybe leave the texting for later).
- **Traffic management on steroids:** AI can analyze traffic patterns in real-time, optimizing traffic flow and reducing congestion. This means less time stuck in rush hour traffic and more time… well, for whatever you actually want to do with your life.

This is just a taste of how AI is transforming our world. It's not about robots taking over (although, that would make a great movie plot), but rather about AI working alongside us to make things faster, easier, and more efficient. Stay tuned for the next part, where we'll explore how AI is impacting even more industries, from education to manufacturing (and maybe even convince your refrigerator to finally tell you why the milk always goes bad before the expiration date).

Chapter 2:
AI in Action: Transforming Our World (Part 3) - From Smarter Schools to Spooky Security Systems: AI is Everywhere (Except Maybe Your Refrigerator... Still)

We've seen how AI is revolutionizing healthcare, retail, and transportation. But this technological revolution is far-reaching, transforming industries you might not even expect. Fasten your seatbelts (or open your textbooks?), because we're venturing into the exciting world of AI in:

Education: From Textbooks to Personalized Learning

Remember those nights spent cramming for exams, desperately memorizing facts that seemed to vanish the moment you left the test room? AI is here to transform education from rote memorization to a more engaging and personalized experience. Here's how:

- **Tailored learning plans:** AI algorithms can analyze a student's strengths and weaknesses, creating personalized learning plans that cater to their individual needs. Imagine having a virtual tutor who adjusts their teaching style just for you, making learning more effective and (dare we say) even fun!

- **Smart grading and feedback:** AI-powered tools can automate the grading process, freeing up teachers' time to focus on what they do best: guiding and mentoring students. Plus, AI can provide students with immediate and personalized feedback on their work, helping them learn from their mistakes and improve faster.

Manufacturing: From Assembly Lines to Smart Factories

Imagine factories that run with incredible efficiency, robots working seamlessly alongside humans, and products manufactured with pinpoint precision. This is the future of manufacturing powered by AI! Get ready for:

- **Predictive maintenance:** AI can analyze sensor data from machines to predict potential failures before they happen. This means less downtime for repairs and a smoother production process.
- **Robots on the assembly line (but not taking your job... yet):** AI-powered robots can handle repetitive tasks with incredible accuracy and speed, freeing up human workers to focus on more complex tasks that require creativity and problem-solving skills. Think of robots as tireless teammates, not job stealers!

Security: From Guard Dogs to AI-powered Surveillance

Keeping things safe and secure is paramount. And AI is emerging as a powerful tool in the security industry. Here's a glimpse into the future:

- **Facial recognition and anomaly detection:** AI can analyze video footage to identify suspicious activity and potential security threats. Imagine a world where security systems can recognize wanted criminals or detect unusual behavior in real-time, helping to prevent crime before it happens.
- **Cybersecurity on steroids:** AI algorithms can analyze vast amounts of data to identify and prevent cyberattacks. Think of AI as a digital bodyguard, constantly on the lookout for threats to your data and systems.

Chapter 2:
AI in Action: Transforming Our World (Part 4) - A Peek into the AI-Powered Future: From Leisure to Agriculture (and Maybe Even Your Refrigerator, Eventually)

We've rocketed through healthcare, retail, transportation, education, manufacturing, and security, witnessing the transformative power of AI. But buckle up, because our journey isn't over yet! Let's explore how AI is infiltrating the world of entertainment and agriculture, and maybe even catch a glimpse into your future smart kitchen (although the self-driving grocery delivery truck might have to wait a bit longer).

Entertainment: From Binge-Watching to Personalized Playlists on Autopilot

Remember the frustration of scrolling endlessly through streaming services, paralyzed by indecision? AI can be your entertainment guru, curating movies, shows, and music tailored to your specific tastes. Here's the future of entertainment with AI:

- **Kiss decision fatigue goodbye:** Imagine AI algorithms analyzing your viewing habits and music preferences to recommend content you'll genuinely enjoy. No more endless scrolling, just seamless entertainment experiences that cater to your mood.
- **Beyond recommendations:** AI-powered immersion: Picture games that adapt to your skill level, virtual reality experiences that feel eerily real, or even personalized storytellers crafting narratives based on your preferences. AI is pushing the boundaries of entertainment, creating experiences that are more engaging and immersive than ever before.

Agriculture: From Backbreaking Labor to Smart Farming Revolution

Farming is a demanding profession, requiring constant monitoring and adaptation to the whims of Mother Nature. But AI is emerging as a powerful tool for farmers, helping them optimize their yields and manage resources more effectively.

- **Precision agriculture takes root:** AI can analyze data from sensors peppered across fields, monitoring soil conditions, water usage, and crop health. This allows farmers to apply fertilizer and water precisely where it's needed, leading to increased yields and reduced waste.
- **Weather prediction and disease prevention go high-tech:** Forget relying on hunches! AI algorithms can analyze historical weather data and current conditions to predict potential weather events and outbreaks of disease. This allows farmers to take preventative measures and protect their precious crops.

The Future of AI: From Your Smartphone to Your Refrigerator (Eventually)

This glimpse into AI's transformative power is just the tip of the iceberg. As technology advances, we can expect AI to become even more integrated into our daily lives. Here's a peek at what the future might hold:

- **Your smart refrigerator (but maybe not just yet):** Imagine a refrigerator that analyzes your eating habits and orders groceries you're about to run out of. (Though, perhaps the self-driving grocery delivery truck can wait a bit longer for safety reasons.)
- **Your AI-powered personal assistant (beyond scheduling meetings):** Picture an AI assistant that manages your schedule, helps you learn a new language,

or even writes you a killer poem for your next date (although, a dash of human charm might still be necessary!).

The possibilities are truly endless. AI is here to stay, and it's up to us to ensure it's used for good. In the next chapter, we'll shift gears and explore the challenges and ethical considerations surrounding AI development. We'll discuss concerns about job displacement, privacy issues, and the potential for bias in AI algorithms. But more importantly, we'll explore ways to ensure AI is developed and used responsibly, shaping a future where this powerful technology benefits all of humanity. So, stay tuned as we delve deeper into the fascinating world of AI!

Chapter 3:
The Road Ahead: Opportunities and Challenges of the AI Revolution

We've explored the incredible potential of AI, from revolutionizing healthcare to personalizing entertainment. But the AI revolution isn't without its challenges. Here, we'll navigate the road ahead, exploring both the exciting opportunities and the potential pitfalls that lie on the horizon.

Part 1: A World of Opportunity

AI presents a multitude of opportunities that can benefit humanity in profound ways:

1. Enhanced Productivity and Efficiency: Imagine AI automating time-consuming tasks across industries, freeing up human workers to focus on creativity, innovation, and problem-solving. This could lead to a significant boost in productivity and efficiency across the board.

2. Personalized Experiences: From healthcare to education, AI can tailor experiences to individual needs. Doctors can leverage AI to provide more personalized treatment plans, while educators can use AI-powered platforms to create customized learning experiences for each student.

3. Scientific Breakthroughs: AI can analyze vast amounts of data and identify patterns that humans might miss, accelerating scientific progress in fields like medicine, materials science, and climate change.

4. Improved Decision-Making: AI algorithms can analyze complex data sets and provide valuable insights to inform decision-making in areas like business, finance, and government.

5. Global Problem-Solving: AI can be a powerful tool for tackling some of humanity's biggest challenges, from climate change and resource management to poverty alleviation and disaster response.

Part 2: Challenges and Ethical Considerations

Despite its potential, AI development raises significant concerns that need to be addressed:

1. Job Displacement: Automation through AI is a double-edged sword. While it can create new jobs, it also has the potential to displace some workers. We need to develop strategies for retraining and reskilling the workforce to navigate this changing landscape.

2. Privacy Concerns: As AI becomes more integrated into our lives, it raises concerns about data privacy and security. We need to establish robust regulations to ensure responsible data collection and usage.

3. Bias in AI Algorithms: AI algorithms are only as good as the data they're trained on. If the data is biased, the algorithms will be biased too. We need to be aware of these biases and develop strategies to mitigate them.

4. The "Black Box" Problem: Some AI systems are complex and opaque, making it difficult to understand how they reach their decisions. This lack of transparency can raise concerns about accountability and fairness.

5. The Ethics of Artificial sentience: While still a topic of science fiction, the possibility of AI achieving sentience raises profound ethical questions about the rights and responsibilities of artificial intelligence.

Conclusion: Shaping the Future of AI

The AI revolution is upon us. The opportunities are vast, but so are the challenges. By embracing a future-oriented mindset, fostering open dialogue, and prioritizing ethical considerations, we can ensure that AI is developed and used responsibly, creating a future where this powerful technology benefits all of humanity.

In the next chapter, we'll explore how you can prepare yourself for the AI revolution. We'll discuss ways to develop your AI literacy, cultivate essential skills for the future, and become an active participant in shaping a responsible and beneficial AI future.

The Most Important Section of The Book Is Coming Now!

You Have To Master The Chapter 4 To Apply Chapter 5

Chapter 4:
You and the AI Revolution: Are You Ready?

The self-driving car whizzes past your window, and a notification pops up on your phone from your AI assistant reminding you to pick up groceries on your way home. The world around us is brimming with AI, and it's only going to become more integrated into our lives. But are you prepared to navigate this exciting, yet sometimes complex, technological revolution?

Developing Your AI Literacy

The first step towards conquering the AI revolution is understanding it. Here's how you can boost your AI literacy and become an informed participant in the future:

1. **Become a Bookworm (of the AI variety):** Dive into the fascinating world of AI by exploring books and articles written by experts in the field. This very book you're holding is a great start, but there's a whole library of knowledge waiting to be discovered. Look for resources that explain AI concepts in a clear and engaging way, even if you don't have a background in technology.
2. **Level Up with Online Courses:** The internet is a treasure trove of educational resources. Many universities and online platforms offer introductory courses on AI. These courses can provide a structured learning experience, taking you from the basics of AI to more advanced concepts. Enrolling in an online course allows you to learn at your own pace and convenience.
3. **Follow the AI Gurus:** Stay on the cutting edge of AI advancements by following the thought leaders shaping the field. Connect with AI researchers, industry experts, and social media influencers who share insights and spark

discussions about AI. Subscribing to their newsletters or following them on social media can keep you up-to-date on the latest developments and different perspectives on AI.

By taking these steps, you'll be well on your way to developing a strong foundation in AI literacy. In the next part of this chapter, we'll explore essential skills you can cultivate to thrive in the AI era. So, stay tuned as we delve deeper into what it takes to be ready for the exciting world of AI!

Cultivating Essential Skills for the AI Era

The AI revolution promises exciting opportunities, but it also presents challenges. While AI automates some tasks, it creates a demand for new skillsets. So, how can you equip yourself for success in this evolving landscape? Here are some key skills to cultivate:

1. **Become a Master Problem-Solver (AI Assistant Not Included):** AI excels at data analysis and pattern recognition, but it can't replace human ingenuity. Honing your critical thinking and problem-solving skills will be crucial. Practice approaching challenges from different angles, brainstorming creative solutions, and thinking outside the box. In a world increasingly reliant on AI, the ability to think critically will be a valuable asset.
2. **Communication and Collaboration: The Human Touch Endures:** While AI can analyze data and generate reports, it lacks the human ability to communicate effectively and collaborate with others. The ability to clearly articulate ideas, actively listen, and work seamlessly with a team (human or AI-powered) will be essential for success. Focus on refining your communication skills, both written and verbal, and

develop a collaborative spirit to thrive in the future workplace.
3. **Embrace Change and Lifelong Learning:** The world of AI is constantly evolving. New advancements emerge all the time, and the skills needed to navigate this landscape will continue to develop. The key to success lies in cultivating a growth mindset and a commitment to lifelong learning. Be open to new ideas, embrace opportunities to learn new skills, and stay curious about the ever-changing world of AI.
4. **Unlock the Power of Data (Without Getting Lost in the Numbers):** Data is the fuel that drives AI. As AI becomes more integrated into our lives, understanding how to analyze and interpret data will be a valuable skill. This doesn't mean becoming a data scientist, but familiarizing yourself with basic data analysis tools and learning how to interpret data visualizations can empower you to make informed decisions based on evidence, not just intuition.

These are just a few essential skills to cultivate as we navigate the AI era. In the next part of this chapter, we'll explore ways you can leverage AI in your daily life, turning science fiction into reality. So, stay tuned as we unlock the practical applications of AI and empower you to become an active participant in the AI revolution! (We will give you some tips and practical applications that you can earn passive income or start your own business based on AI technologies.)

But to do any of those actions above you have to understand what we are really up to. And the technology that will help you start a business or earn passive income. Please pay attention to this section. First improve your pre required skills mentioned in chapter 4. Just after you feel ready start chapter 5.

Leveraging AI in Your Daily Life

The concept of AI assistants and self-driving cars might seem futuristic, but AI is already woven into the fabric of our daily lives. Here's how you can leverage the power of AI to enhance your productivity, well-being, and decision-making:

1. **Become a Productivity Powerhouse with AI Tools:** Feeling overwhelmed by to-do lists and an overflowing inbox? AI can be your secret weapon. Utilize AI-powered task management apps like Asana or Todoist to stay organized, set priorities, and meet deadlines. Explore AI-powered calendars like Calendly or X.ai to schedule meetings efficiently and free up your time for more strategic work.

    I also use Notion for almost every single thing! I defined a function for almost every single planning and habit based action. I will share some of my Notion templates later on.

2. **Transform Learning into a Personalized Adventure:** Gone are the days of rote memorization and one-size-fits-all learning styles. AI-powered learning platforms like Duolingo or Coursera can personalize your education, cater to your learning pace, and identify areas where you need extra support. Imagine learning a new language through interactive exercises tailored to your specific needs, or mastering a new skill through an AI-powered platform that adjusts its difficulty based on your progress.

3. **Unlock Your Health Potential with AI Assistance:** AI can be a valuable partner in your health and wellness journey. Utilize AI-powered fitness trackers like Fitbit or Strava to monitor your activity levels and set achievable goals. Explore AI-powered sleep tracking apps like Sleep Cycle or Pillow to analyze your sleep patterns and

improve your sleep quality. Remember, AI-powered health assistants cannot replace medical professionals, but they can be a handy tool for monitoring your well-being and making informed decisions about your health.
4. **Make Data-Driven Decisions with AI Insights:** Stop relying solely on gut instinct! Leverage AI-powered research tools to gather data and gain insights relevant to your personal or professional life. Imagine researching a new investment opportunity and utilizing an AI-powered platform to analyze market trends and identify potential risks. While AI shouldn't replace your judgment entirely, it can empower you to make more informed decisions backed by data.

These are just a few examples of how AI can be a powerful tool to improve our daily lives. As AI technology continues to evolve, we can expect even more innovative applications to emerge. The key lies in approaching AI with a curious mind and a willingness to explore its potential.

In the final part of this chapter, we'll issue a call to action, encouraging you to become an active participant in shaping a future where AI benefits all of humanity. This part will play an important role as well. So pay attention!

Conclusion

The AI revolution is upon us, and it's not just about self-driving cars and robots taking over our jobs (although those might be coming down the line). It's about a new era where intelligent machines can augment our capabilities and empower us to solve some of the world's most pressing challenges. But this exciting future hinges on responsible development and ensuring AI is used for good. So, how can you, the reader, become an active participant in shaping a future where AI benefits all?

Embrace the Power of "Both/And," Not "Either/Or"

The future isn't about humans versus machines. It's about humans and machines working together. Focus on developing the skills that complement AI, not compete with it. Cultivate your creativity, critical thinking, and emotional intelligence – areas where humans will always have an edge.

Become an Advocate for Responsible AI

The potential of AI is vast, but so are the challenges. Stay informed about the ethical considerations surrounding AI development, such as bias in algorithms and potential job displacement. Here's how you can advocate for responsible AI:

- **Follow AI news and updates:** Stay current on the latest advancements and potential pitfalls of AI by following reputable news sources and research institutions that cover AI.
- **Engage in discussions about AI ethics:** Don't be afraid to spark conversations about AI ethics with friends, family, colleagues, or even online communities. Share your concerns and encourage others to think critically about the responsible development and use of AI.
- **Support organizations working on AI ethics:** There are numerous organizations dedicated to ensuring AI is developed and used ethically. Consider researching these organizations, such as the Partnership on AI or the Algorithmic Justice League, and see how you can contribute through volunteering, donating, or simply staying informed about their work.

Be a Force for Positive Change

Don't just be a passive observer of the AI revolution. Become an active participant! Explore ways to leverage AI for good in your community. Here are some ideas to get you started:

- **Think about local challenges:** Identify issues or areas for improvement in your community, such as education, healthcare, or environmental protection. Then, research how AI-powered solutions might be able to address these challenges.
- **Get involved in AI-focused initiatives:** Look for local hackathons, workshops, or community events related to AI. Participating in these events can allow you to connect with like-minded individuals, brainstorm ideas, and even contribute to the development of positive AI applications.
- **Become an AI innovator:** Do you have a brilliant idea for how AI can be used to improve a specific aspect of life? Don't let it stay just an idea! Consider pursuing an education in AI, participating in hackathons focused on social good, or even starting your own project to develop an AI-powered solution for a cause you care about.

The Future is Yours to Shape

The AI revolution is a journey, not a destination. By developing your AI literacy, cultivating essential skills, and leveraging AI responsibly, you can become a powerful force for positive change. Let's work together to ensure that AI becomes a tool that empowers humanity to create a brighter future for all.

Call to Action: Your AI Adventure Continues

This is just the beginning of your AI adventure. Here are some specific ways you can continue your journey and become an active participant in shaping the future of AI:

- **Explore online resources:** Dive deeper into the world of AI by exploring websites, articles, podcasts, and documentaries dedicated to AI. Here are a few resources to get you started:

- **Websites:** The Future of Life Institute (https://futureoflife.org/), Partnership on AI (https://partnershiponai.org/)
- **Articles:** "21 Must-Read Articles on Artificial Intelligence" by MIT Technology Review (https://www.technologyreview.com/topic/artificial-intelligence/)
- **Podcasts:** "Lex Fridman Podcast" (https://lexfridman.com/podcast/), "Machine Learning Guide Podcast" (https://ocdevel.com/mlg)
- **Documentaries:** "AI: For Good or Evil?" by PBS (https://www.pbs.org/video/the-future-of-ai-1708554067/), "AlphaGo" by DeepMind (https://www.youtube.com/watch?v=WXuK6gekU1Y)

- **Engage in discussions:** Talk to friends, family, and colleagues about AI. Share what you've learned, discuss your thoughts and concerns, and be open to hearing different perspectives. Social media groups or online forums focused on AI can also be great places to engage in discussions.
- **Support organizations working on responsible AI:** As mentioned earlier, numerous organizations are dedicated to ensuring responsible AI development. Here's how you can get involved and support their work:
  - **Volunteer your time:** Many organizations welcome volunteers with diverse skillsets. Offer your time and expertise in areas like writing, graphic design, web development, or even just spreading awareness about their initiatives.
  - **Donate:** If you can't spare time to volunteer, consider making a financial contribution to support the

ongoing work of organizations promoting responsible AI. Every bit helps!
- **Become an ambassador:** Become a vocal advocate for responsible AI in your own network. Share information from these organizations, attend their events (online or in-person), and encourage others to learn more about and support their work.

- **Become an AI innovator:** Do you have an idea for how AI can be used for good? Don't let it languish! Here are some ways to turn your idea into reality:
  - **Pursue an education in AI:** Consider taking online courses, enrolling in a degree program, or attending workshops to develop your AI skills and knowledge. There are numerous educational resources available for all levels, from beginners to those seeking advanced training.
  - **Participate in hackathons:** Many hackathons focus on developing AI solutions for social good. Participating in these events allows you to collaborate with other passionate individuals, brainstorm ideas, and even compete for funding to develop your AI project.
  - **Develop your own AI solution:** If you have the technical skills, consider diving headfirst and developing your own AI-powered solution. Start small, focus on a specific problem you'd like to address, and gradually build your project. There are many open-source AI libraries and resources available online to help you get started.

The future of AI is in our hands. By taking action and becoming an active participant, you can help ensure that AI is used for good and empowers all of humanity. Let's embark on this AI adventure together and create a brighter future for all!

Chapter 5: Unleashing the Power of AI: Your Gateway to Passive Income!

Get ready to unlock a treasure chest of opportunity! In this chapter, we'll delve into the exciting world of AI-powered passive income. Forget the nine-to-five grind; imagine a future where intelligent machines handle the heavy lifting, while you reap the rewards. AI is no longer just science fiction; it's a powerful tool waiting to be harnessed by anyone with a curious mind and an entrepreneurial spirit. So, buckle up and get ready for a dose of inspiration as we explore real-life success stories and practical roadmaps to turn your AI dreams into reality!

From Etsy Shop to AI Powerhouse: The Story of Sarah and Her Personalized Jewelry Line

Sarah, a passionate jewelry designer, poured her heart into her Etsy shop. But the time commitment of managing orders, marketing, and customer service left her feeling burnt out. Enter AI! Sarah discovered a platform that utilized AI to analyze customer preferences and design trends. She integrated this AI tool into her shop, allowing her to create personalized jewelry pieces based on individual customer data. The results? Sarah's sales skyrocketed, her workload decreased, and she could finally focus on the creative aspects of her business she loved.

From Struggling Musician to AI-powered Composer: The Rise of David

David, a talented musician, dreamt of creating music that resonated with a wider audience. However, the traditional music industry proved challenging. Then, he stumbled upon an AI-powered music composition tool. This innovative platform allowed him to collaborate with AI to create unique and engaging music pieces. David used the AI-generated compositions as a foundation, adding his own creative flair to personalize the sound. Within months, his music gained traction online, leading to record deals and a flourishing career – all fueled by the power of AI!

These are just a few examples of how ordinary people are leveraging AI to achieve extraordinary results. The possibilities are truly endless! Imagine developing an AI-powered language tutor that personalizes learning for students around the world, or creating an AI-driven stock analysis tool that empowers individuals to make informed investment decisions. The key lies in identifying a problem, recognizing the potential of AI to solve it, and taking that first step towards building your passive income dream.

Get Ready to Be Amazed: A Sneak Peek into the Future of AI and Passive Income

The future of AI-powered passive income is brimming with exciting possibilities. Here's a glimpse of what's to come:

- **AI-powered content creation:** Imagine AI generating high-quality blog posts, social media content, or even scripts for your YouTube channel, freeing up your time for strategy and promotion.
- **Hyper-personalized learning platforms:** AI tutors that tailor learning experiences to individual student needs, creating a revolution in online education.
- **AI-driven stock analysis tools:** Imagine AI algorithms providing in-depth market insights and personalized investment recommendations, empowering individuals to navigate the financial landscape with confidence.
- **AI-powered customer service chatbots:** Say goodbye to long wait times! AI chatbots will handle basic customer

inquiries efficiently, freeing up human representatives for more complex issues.

The world of AI-powered passive income is waiting to be explored. Are you ready to join the revolution? Let's turn the page and embark on your AI income adventure! (This line acts as a transition point to Part 1, where we'll delve into the "why" behind AI for passive income and explore specific business ideas)

Why AI Makes Passive Income Your Superpower

The stories of Sarah and David showcase the transformative power of AI for passive income. But why exactly is AI such a game-changer in this realm? Here are a few reasons why AI can be your secret weapon for building a steady stream of income without the constant hustle:

1. Automation is Your Superpower: Repetitive tasks are the bane of any passive income venture. AI thrives on automation, taking over the mundane aspects of your business and freeing you to focus on strategy, growth, and innovation. Imagine an AI system managing your online store, automatically processing orders, handling customer inquiries, and even generating personalized product recommendations. You get to enjoy the profits while AI takes care of the day-to-day operations.

2. Scalability Made Simple: One of the biggest challenges with traditional passive income streams is scalability. With AI, however, scaling becomes effortless. Once you've developed your AI-powered system, it can handle an increasing workload without requiring additional manpower. This means your income potential has virtually no ceiling. Imagine an AI-powered content creation tool you develop – the more users who subscribe, the more revenue you generate, without needing to personally create each piece of content.

3. Data-Driven Decisions, Skyrocketing Results: AI thrives on data analysis. By leveraging AI, you can gain valuable insights into your target audience, market trends, and customer behavior. This data empowers you to make informed decisions about your business, optimize your strategies, and ultimately maximize your passive income potential. Imagine an AI-powered stock analysis tool you create – the data analysis capabilities of AI can help users identify investment opportunities they might have missed on their own, leading to potentially higher returns.

4. The Power of Personalization: In today's crowded marketplace, personalization is key to standing out. AI excels at creating customized experiences for users. Imagine an AI-powered language learning app that tailors lessons to individual learning styles and preferences, leading to higher engagement and ultimately, recurring subscriptions.

5. 24/7 Work Ethic (Without the Burnout): Unlike humans, AI doesn't need sleep or breaks. Your AI-powered system can work tirelessly around the clock, generating income even while you're catching up on sleep or pursuing other ventures.

By harnessing the power of automation, scalability, data-driven insights, personalization, and a tireless work ethic, AI can be the ultimate force multiplier for your passive income goals. In the next part, we'll dive into the exciting world of specific AI-powered business ideas that you can launch, even with limited resources. So, get ready to unleash your inner AI entrepreneur and unlock the door to financial freedom!

20 AI-Powered Business Ideas for Passive Income (Even with No Money!)

The world of AI is bursting with possibilities for passive income generation. Here are 20 ideas to spark your entrepreneurial spirit, some requiring minimal investment and perfect for beginners:

Free or Low-Cost Ideas:

1. **AI-powered Content Creation Assistant:** Train a large language model (like Bard!) to generate blog post outlines, social media captions, or product descriptions. This frees up your time for editing, content strategy, and promotion.
2. **Virtual Assistant with an AI Edge:** Offer virtual assistant services that leverage AI for tasks like appointment scheduling, email management, or lead nurturing through chatbots.
3. **AI-powered Stock Market Analysis (Disclaimer: Informational purposes only):** Utilize free or low-cost AI tools to analyze market trends and identify potential investment opportunities. Remember, this shouldn't be taken as financial advice!
4. **Freelance AI Tutoring:** Offer online tutoring services where you leverage AI-powered learning platforms to personalize lessons and cater to individual student needs.
5. **AI-powered Social Media Scheduler and Content Generator:** Create a service that utilizes AI to schedule social media posts, analyze audience engagement, and even generate creative content for various platforms.
6. **AI-powered E-commerce Recommendation Engine:** Develop a plugin or service that integrates with e-commerce platforms, using AI to recommend products to customers based on their browsing history and purchase behavior.
7. **AI-powered Data Analysis and Reporting Service:** Offer businesses an affordable AI-powered service to analyze their data, generate reports, and identify

actionable insights to improve operations or marketing strategies.
8. **AI-powered Transcription Service:** Leverage AI transcription tools to offer transcription services for meetings, interviews, or lectures.
9. **AI-powered Translation Assistant:** Create a platform that utilizes AI to translate documents, emails, or websites into multiple languages, catering to a global audience.
10. **AI-powered Music Playlist Generator:** Develop a platform that uses AI to curate personalized music playlists based on user preferences, mood, or activity (work, workout, relaxation).

Ideas Requiring Some Investment:

11. **Develop an AI-powered Language Learning App:** Design an app that uses AI to personalize language learning for users, offering customized exercises, real-time feedback, and interactive practice sessions.
12. **Create an AI-powered Stock Photo Service:** Train an AI to generate unique and high-quality stock photos that cater to specific needs and niches (think travel, food, business concepts).
13. **Build an AI-powered Music Composition Tool:** Develop a platform that allows users to create personalized music pieces with the help of AI algorithms. Let users choose genres, instruments, and moods to generate unique compositions.
14. **Launch an AI-powered Fitness Coaching App:** Design an app that utilizes AI to create personalized workout plans based on fitness goals and user data. The AI can track progress, provide motivational feedback, and curate workout routines.

15. **Develop an AI-powered Chatbot for Customer Service:** Create a chatbot powered by AI that can answer customer queries 24/7, resolve basic issues, and even personalize the customer service experience by remembering past interactions.
16. **Design an AI-powered Creative Writing Assistant:** Develop a tool that assists writers with overcoming writer's block, suggesting plot points, generating character descriptions, or even creating outlines based on initial story ideas.
17. **Build an AI-powered Cybersecurity Threat Detection System:** Develop a software solution that utilizes AI to detect and prevent cyberattacks for small and medium businesses.
18. **Create an AI-powered Legal Research Assistant:** Design a platform that leverages AI to assist lawyers and legal professionals with legal research, analyzing case law, and identifying relevant precedents.
19. **Develop an AI-powered Real Estate Market Analysis Tool:** Create a tool that analyzes real estate data using AI to predict market trends, identify undervalued properties, and empower investors to make informed decisions.
20. **Build an AI-powered Travel Itinerary Planner:** Design a platform that utilizes AI to personalize travel itineraries based on user preferences, budget, and travel style, suggesting destinations, attractions, and activities for a unique and unforgettable experience.

Remember, this is just the beginning! The possibilities for AI-powered passive income are endless. With creativity and dedication, you can transform your ideas into reality and unlock a future of financial freedom. In Part 3, we'll equip you with a roadmap to turn your AI business dream into a thriving venture. Stay tuned!

Here are top 3 easiest business models -Author's selections- you can start free to low cost and in no time:

1. AI-powered Content Creation Assistant: Your Secret Weapon for Effortless Content

Ever feel bogged down by the constant need to create fresh content for your blog, social media, or website? Imagine a reliable assistant who can churn out blog post outlines, craft catchy social media captions, or even generate product descriptions – all powered by AI! This is the magic of the AI-powered content creation assistant model, one of the simplest and most beginner-friendly ways to step into the world of AI-powered passive income.

Why it's so Simple:

The beauty of this model lies in its accessibility. You don't need to be a coding whiz or an AI developer. Several free and low-cost large language models (LLMs) are readily available online, like Bard here at Google AI! These LLMs can be trained and customized to understand your writing style and content needs.

Pros:

- **Low Barrier to Entry:** No coding skills or technical expertise required. Many free or low-cost LLMs exist.
- **Time-Saving Efficiency:** Automate repetitive tasks like content ideation and outline creation. Focus on strategy and editing.
- **Scalability:** Easily scale your content creation efforts as your business grows.
- **Flexibility:** Work from anywhere, anytime with an internet connection.

Cons:

- **Learning Curve:** While user-friendly, there's a learning curve to training and effectively utilizing the LLM.
- **AI-Generated Content Needs Editing:** Don't expect perfect, polished content right away. Human editing remains crucial.
- **Limited Creativity:** LLMs excel at replicating existing styles but might struggle with highly creative content.

How to Get Started:

1. **Choose Your LLM:** Research free or low-cost LLM options like Bard (Google AI), ChatGPT (OpenAI), or Rytr. Each offers unique features and pricing plans.
2. **Train Your AI Assistant:** Provide your chosen LLM with samples of your writing style, content topics, and desired tone. The more data you feed it, the better it understands your needs.
3. **Experiment and Refine:** Start with simple tasks like generating headlines or product descriptions. Gradually progress to more complex tasks like blog post outlines. Refine your prompts and instructions based on the results.

Where to Start:

You can kickstart your AI-powered content creation business from the comfort of your home! All you need is a computer with an internet connection and access to your chosen LLM platform.

Equipment:

- Computer with internet access
- Account with your chosen LLM platform

Alternative Options:

- If free or low-cost LLM options don't meet your needs, explore paid LLM services with more advanced features.
- Consider offering additional content creation services like editing, proofreading, or content strategy development alongside your AI-powered assistance.

Useful Sources:

- Bard Documentation: https://gemini.google.com/
- ChatGPT OpenAI: https://openai.com/chatgpt
- Rytr: https://rytr.me/ - (This is just an example, there are many other LLM options available)

How Much Can You Make?

The earning potential varies depending on the content you create, your target audience, and the value you offer. Here's a rough estimate:

- Social media captions: $10-$25 per caption
- Blog post outlines: $25-$50 per outline
- Product descriptions: $10-$20 per description

Remember, consistency and quality are key to building a successful AI-powered content creation business. As you refine your skills and establish a client base, your earning potential can grow significantly.

2. Virtual Assistant with an AI Edge: Automate Tasks, Boost Productivity

Feeling overwhelmed by the ever-growing to-do list for your virtual assistant business? Wish you could streamline repetitive tasks and free up your time to focus on high-value services? The virtual assistant with an AI edge model offers the perfect solution! By integrating AI tools into your existing virtual assistant skillset, you can expand your service offerings, improve efficiency, and ultimately serve a wider range of clients.

Why it's so Simple:

This model leverages your existing virtual assistant skills and combines them with the power of AI. You don't need to be an AI expert – focusing on utilizing user-friendly AI tools designed to automate specific tasks is key.

Pros:

- **Builds on Existing Skills:** No need to learn a completely new skillset. Leverage your virtual assistant expertise.
- **Increased Efficiency:** AI automates repetitive tasks, freeing up your time for client interaction and strategic thinking.
- **Enhanced Service Offerings:** Expand your service portfolio with AI-powered features like appointment scheduling or email management chatbots.
- **Greater Scalability:** Handle a larger client base with increased efficiency thanks to AI automation.

Cons:

- **Staying Updated:** Keeping pace with the evolving landscape of AI tools requires ongoing research and learning.
- **Client Education:** Some clients might require explanation and reassurance about the role of AI in your services.
- **Limited Customization:** AI tools might not offer complete customization for highly specific client needs.

How to Get Involved:

1. **Identify Repetitive Tasks:** Analyze your current virtual assistant workflow. Pinpoint tasks that are repetitive and

well-suited for automation, like scheduling appointments, managing email inboxes, or data entry.
2. **Research AI Tools:** Explore AI tools designed specifically for virtual assistants. Popular options include Calendly (scheduling), ManyChat (chatbots), or Zapier (automations).
3. **Experiment and Integrate:** Start by testing a single AI tool for a specific task. Integrate it into your workflow and monitor its effectiveness.
4. **Client Communication:** Be transparent with your clients about how AI tools assist you. Highlight the benefits of increased efficiency and focus on tasks requiring your human expertise.

Where to Start:

You can launch your AI-powered virtual assistant service from your home office! All you need is a computer with an internet connection, your virtual assistant management tools, and access to chosen AI platforms.

Equipment:

- Computer with internet connection
- Virtual assistant management software (optional)
- Accounts with chosen AI platforms for tasks like scheduling or chatbots

Alternative Options:

- If you're new to the virtual assistant world, consider starting with basic virtual assistant services and gradually integrate AI tools as you gain experience.
- Explore offering specialized virtual assistant services for specific industries, like real estate or e-commerce.

Useful Sources:

- Calendly: https://calendly.com/
- ManyChat: https://manychat.com/
- Zapier: https://zapier.com/

How Much Can You Make?

Virtual assistant rates vary based on experience, location, and offered services. Here's a general guideline:

- Basic virtual assistant services: $15-$25 per hour
- Virtual assistant services with AI integration: $20-$30 per hour
- Specialized virtual assistant services: $25-$40 per hour

By incorporating AI tools and expanding your service offerings, you can significantly increase your earning potential as an AI-powered virtual assistant.

Finding Clients:

- **Freelance Platforms:** Sign up on popular freelance platforms like Upwork or Fiverr and create a profile highlighting your virtual assistant skills and AI expertise.
- **Social Media Marketing:** Build a strong presence on social media platforms like LinkedIn or Facebook. Target entrepreneurs and small businesses, showcasing the benefits of AI-powered virtual assistance.
- **Networking:** Attend industry events or online communities for virtual assistants. Network with other VAs and explore potential collaborations or referrals.
- **Cold Emailing:** Research small businesses that could benefit from your services and craft personalized cold emails showcasing your value proposition.

Convincing Your First Client (Without References):

- **Focus on Value Proposition:** Clearly articulate the benefits of AI-powered virtual assistance. Explain how it saves them time, improves efficiency, and allows them to focus on core business activities.
- **Offer Free Trial/Consultation:** Provide a free trial period or consultation to showcase your skills and the effectiveness of AI integration. This builds trust and allows them to experience the benefits firsthand.
- **Case Studies/Testimonials (Even if Hypothetical):** Develop hypothetical case studies showcasing how AI-powered VA services helped similar businesses. While you might not have real references yet, these examples demonstrate the potential impact.
- **Highlight Transferable Skills:** Leverage any relevant experience you have, even if it's not directly in virtual assistance. Strong organizational skills, project management experience, or customer service expertise can be valuable assets.
- **Focus on Learning Agility:** Emphasize your eagerness to learn and adapt to new technologies. Demonstrate your commitment to staying updated with the latest AI tools and their applications in the virtual assistant world.
- **Competitive Rates:** Consider offering competitive rates, especially when starting out. This can incentivize clients to take a chance on you, knowing they have minimal financial risk.
- **Over-deliver and Build Trust:** Go the extra mile to exceed your client's expectations. Deliver high-quality work, meet deadlines consistently, and be proactive in identifying areas where AI automation can further benefit their business.

Building trust and showcasing your value as an AI-powered virtual assistant is key to securing your first client. By focusing on the benefits you offer, demonstrating your skills and dedication, and being transparent about your experience level, you can position yourself as a valuable asset for potential clients, even without a long list of references.

3. AI-Powered Social Media Management: Effortless Engagement for Busy Businesses

Do you have a knack for social media and understand the power of online engagement? Social media management can be a demanding task, especially for small businesses struggling to keep up with multiple platforms and ever-changing algorithms. This is where the AI-powered social media management model comes in! By leveraging AI tools, you can offer businesses a powerful solution to streamline their social media presence, increase engagement, and ultimately drive results.

Why it's so Simple:

This model capitalizes on your existing social media knowledge and combines it with the automation capabilities of AI. Several user-friendly AI platforms can help with tasks like scheduling posts, analyzing audience engagement metrics, and even generating creative content ideas.

Pros:

- **Leverages Existing Skills:** No coding expertise required. Build on your social media knowledge and understanding of online communities.
- **Automates Time-Consuming Tasks:** Free up your time for strategy and client communication by utilizing AI for scheduling and content generation.
- **Scalability:** Manage multiple social media accounts for various clients efficiently with the help of AI tools.

- **Measurable Results:** Track social media performance metrics and demonstrate the value you deliver to clients through data-driven reports.

Cons:

- Understanding Social Media Landscape: Staying updated on social media trends and algorithm changes is crucial for success.
- **Limited Creative Control:** AI-generated content might require human editing to ensure brand voice and tone consistency.
- **Client Management:** Managing different client needs and expectations for their social media presence requires effective communication.

How to Get Involved:

1. **Sharpen Your Social Media Skills:** Ensure a strong foundation in social media marketing principles, including content creation, audience engagement strategies, and platform-specific algorithms.
2. **Research AI Social Media Tools:** Explore popular AI social media management platforms like Hootsuite, Buffer, or Socialbakers. Each offers different features and functionalities.
3. **Experiment and Refine:** Start by utilizing AI tools for basic tasks like scheduling posts or analyzing audience insights. Gradually integrate more advanced features as you gain confidence.
4. **Build a Social Media Management Portfolio:** Create sample social media strategies or manage personal/dummy accounts to showcase your skills and the effectiveness of AI integration.

Where to Start:

You can launch your AI-powered social media management service from your home office! All you need is a computer with an internet connection, access to chosen AI platforms, and social media management tools (optional).

Equipment:

- Computer with internet connection
- Accounts with chosen AI social media management platforms
- Social media management software (optional)

Alternative Options:

- If you're new to social media management, consider offering basic social media consulting services before integrating AI tools.
- Specialize in a specific niche or industry where you can develop in-depth social media knowledge and cater to targeted clients.

Useful Sources:

- Hootsuite: https://hootsuite.com/
- Buffer: https://buffer.com/
- Socialbakers: https://www.socialbakers.com/

How Much Can You Make?

Social media management rates vary depending on experience, the number of platforms managed, and client needs. Here's a general guideline:

- **Basic social media management:** $500-$1000 per month per client

- **AI-powered social media management:** $750-$1500 per month per client
- **Social media management for large businesses:** $2000+ per month per client

By offering a valuable combination of human expertise and AI automation, you can establish yourself as a sought-after social media management professional and build a successful AI-powered business.

Finding Clients:

- **Freelance Platforms:** Sign up on these popular freelance platforms to create a profile highlighting your social media expertise and AI-powered approach:
  - Upwork: https://www.upwork.com/
  - Fiverr: https://www.fiverr.com/
- **Social Media Marketing:** Build a strong presence on social media platforms like LinkedIn or Twitter. Here are the links:
  - LinkedIn: https://www.linkedin.com/
  - Twitter: https://twitter.com/?lang=en
- **Cold Emailing:** Research small and medium businesses that could benefit from your services. Craft personalized cold emails outlining the challenges they might face with social media management and how your AI-powered approach can solve them.
- **Networking:** Attend industry events or online communities for social media professionals. Network with other marketers and explore potential collaborations or referrals. Look for industry events on platforms like:
  - Eventbrite: https://www.eventbrite.com/

- Meetup: https://www.meetup.com/ (focus on marketing or social media meetups)

Remember tailoring your approach to each platform is key. On freelance platforms, focus on creating a compelling profile that showcases your skills and experience with AI-powered social media management. On social media, engage with potential clients, share valuable content, and establish yourself as a thought leader in the industry. Cold emailing requires crafting personalized messages that target specific needs and demonstrate the value you can deliver. Finally, networking allows you to build relationships with potential clients and industry professionals who might offer referrals or collaboration opportunities.

Convincing Your First Client (Without References):

- **Showcase a Sample Social Media Strategy:** Develop a sample social media strategy tailored to a specific niche or industry, demonstrating your understanding of target audiences and content creation.
- **Free Social Media Audit:** Offer a free social media audit for potential clients. Analyze their current social media presence, identify areas for improvement, and showcase how AI tools can address those challenges.
- **Highlight Measurable Results:** Focus on the data-driven aspects of AI-powered social media management. Explain how you'll track key metrics and generate reports to demonstrate the impact of your strategies.
- **Offer a Trial Period:** Consider providing a limited-time trial period at a reduced rate. This allows clients to experience the benefits of your services firsthand and builds trust before a long-term commitment.
- **Testimonials (Even Hypothetical):** Craft testimonials from satisfied clients (even if hypothetical) based on the sample social media strategy or free audit you offered.

While not real clients, these testimonials demonstrate the potential value you can deliver.

Step-by-Step Example Business Kickstart:

1. **Choose Your Niche:** Decide on a specific industry or niche where you can develop focused social media expertise. This allows you to tailor your services and target ideal clients. (Example: Social media management for health and wellness businesses)
2. **Build Your Skills:** Take online courses, attend workshops, or gain experience by managing personal or dummy social media accounts to hone your social media marketing skills and understanding of different platforms.
3. **Research AI Social Media Tools:** Explore and compare features offered by AI social media management platforms like Hootsuite, Buffer, or Socialbakers. Choose a platform that aligns with your budget and functionalities you need.
4. **Develop a Sample Social Media Strategy:** Craft a sample strategy for your chosen niche, outlining content pillars, target audience engagement tactics, and a posting schedule. Utilize free AI content generation tools to experiment with content ideas.
5. **Create a Portfolio:** Develop a portfolio showcasing your social media expertise. Include the sample strategy, any social media audit reports you've created, and testimonials (even if hypothetical).
6. **Launch Your Online Presence:** Build a website or social media profiles specifically for your AI-powered social media management services. Highlight your skills, showcase your portfolio, and include clear calls to action for potential clients.
7. **Client Acquisition:** Utilize a combination of freelance platforms, social media marketing, cold emailing, and

networking to reach out to potential clients. Focus on the value proposition of your AI-powered approach and the measurable results you can deliver.
8. **Start Small, Scale Up:** Begin by securing a few smaller clients to gain experience and build your confidence. Deliver exceptional service, exceed expectations, and leverage positive client experiences to attract larger clients as you scale your business.

By following these steps, you can transform your social media expertise and AI-powered approach into a thriving social media management business, even without a long list of references to start. Remember, focus on showcasing your value proposition, demonstrating your skills, and building trust with potential clients – this will pave the way for success in the exciting world of AI-powered business.

Launching Your AI-Powered Business: From Idea to Action

Congratulations! You've explored three exciting AI-powered business models that leverage your existing skills and technological advancements. Now, it's time to bridge the gap between concept and reality. Here, we'll delve into the essential steps to take your AI business idea and transform it into a successful venture.

1. Refine Your Business Idea:

- **Market Research:** Before diving in, conduct thorough market research to validate your chosen AI business model. Identify your target audience, understand their needs and pain points, and research any existing competitors offering similar solutions.

- **Value Proposition:** Clearly define the unique value proposition your AI-powered business offers. How will your service make a difference for your target customers?
- **Business Model Canvas:** Utilize a Business Model Canvas to map out your overall business strategy. This one-page framework helps visualize key components like customer segments, revenue streams, and marketing channels. Several online resources and templates are available for free.

2. Develop a Minimum Viable Product (MVP):

- **Start Small:** Don't aim for a perfect, all-encompassing product right away. Instead, focus on developing a Minimum Viable Product (MVP). This is a basic version of your AI-powered service with core functionalities that allows you to gather initial user feedback and iterate based on real-world data.
- **Focus on Core Functionality:** Prioritize the most essential features and functionalities your target audience needs. This ensures your MVP delivers immediate value and helps you identify areas for improvement.
- **Gather Feedback and Refine:** Actively seek feedback from potential customers and beta testers on your MVP. Use this feedback to refine your product, identify any shortcomings, and ensure it effectively addresses your target market's needs.

3. Build Your Brand Identity:

- **Develop a Brand Story:** Craft a compelling brand story that resonates with your target audience. This story should explain your purpose, values, and how your AI-powered business solves customer problems in a unique way.

- **Visual Identity:** Create a professional visual identity that includes a logo, brand colors, and consistent design elements. This visual identity will be reflected in your website, marketing materials, and social media presence.
- **Establish Your Online Presence:** Build a user-friendly website that showcases your services, highlights the benefits of your AI approach, and provides clear calls to action for potential customers.

4. Marketing and Customer Acquisition:

- **Digital Marketing Strategy:** Develop a comprehensive digital marketing strategy to reach your target audience. This might include content marketing, social media marketing, search engine optimization (SEO), or even pay-per-click (PPC) advertising depending on your budget and target market.
- **Content Marketing:** Create valuable and informative content that educates your target audience about the benefits of AI-powered solutions in your chosen field. This establishes you as a thought leader and attracts potential customers organically.
- **Networking and Public Relations:** Network with other professionals and industry influencers. Explore opportunities to speak at events, contribute guest articles to relevant publications, and generate positive press coverage about your AI business.

5. Legal and Financial Considerations:

- **Business Structure:** Choose the most suitable legal structure for your business, such as sole proprietorship, partnership, or Limited Liability Company (LLC). This decision will impact factors like taxes, liability, and ownership.

- **Financial Projections:** Create financial projections to forecast your revenue, expenses, and potential profitability. This will help you secure funding if needed and make informed financial decisions for your business.
- **Compliance Requirements:** Research any legal and regulatory requirements that might pertain to your AI business model. This might involve data privacy regulations or specific industry standards depending on your location and chosen niche.

By following these steps, leveraging the resources available online, and staying updated on the ever-evolving AI landscape, you can turn your innovative idea into a thriving venture that empowers you to be your own boss and make a positive impact with the power of artificial intelligence.

In the next book we are going to dive deeper into AI based businesses. And especially how to fund and manage the business and grow your team. For now this should be enough for you to get involved in business. Select a model above or come up with your own idea according to information provided in chapter 5, and your background. And start in no time. Don't forget knowledge itself means nothing unless you call it to action.

Chapter 6: Unleash Your Inner AI Entrepreneur: Fueling Motivation and Inspiration

The world of AI is brimming with possibilities, waiting for innovative minds like yours to turn them into reality. This chapter serves as your motivational toolkit, packed with resources and inspiration to ignite your passion for building an AI-powered business.

Spark Your Creativity: Reimagine the Future with AI

Take a moment to envision the impact AI could have on your chosen field. Could it automate mundane tasks, personalize user experiences, or even unlock entirely new business models? Challenge yourself to think outside the box. Explore emerging AI trends and advancements, and consider how they might disrupt or revolutionize your industry.

Fueling Your Passion: Inspiration from AI Trailblazers

Sometimes, the best motivation comes from seeing others succeed. Research real-world examples of AI-powered businesses making waves in various sectors. From healthcare chatbots to AI-powered language learning platforms, there's a wealth of inspiration waiting to be discovered.

Here are some resources to get you started:

- **Forbes: Top 50 Artificial Intelligence Companies (2024):** https://www.forbes.com/lists/ai50/
- **MIT Technology Review: AI Innovators Under 35 (2024):** https://www.technologyreview.com/

Beyond Inspiration: Practical Steps to Get Started

Motivation is crucial, but it needs a roadmap to translate into action. Here are some practical steps to kickstart your AI business journey:

- **Validate Your Idea:** Conduct thorough market research to ensure your AI-powered solution addresses a real need. Talk to potential customers, gather feedback, and refine your concept based on the market response.
- **Develop Your Skills:** The world of AI can feel overwhelming. Fortunately, there are numerous online courses, workshops, and even bootcamps dedicated to teaching the fundamentals of AI and its applications in business.
- **Embrace Continuous Learning:** The field of AI is constantly evolving. Commit to lifelong learning and stay updated on the latest trends and advancements to keep your business at the forefront.

Bonus Tip: Leverage the Power of ChatGPT

As you navigate the exciting world of AI, consider using tools like ChatGPT to your advantage. ChatGPT can be a valuable brainstorming partner, helping you generate creative ideas, refine your business plan, or even craft compelling marketing copy.

Remember: The road to building a successful AI business is paved with learning, adaptation, and perseverance. Don't be discouraged by setbacks. Embrace the journey, learn from your experiences, and keep pushing forward with your innovative ideas.

Building Your AI Business Vocabulary

Dictionary of Modern AI Terms

- **AI (Artificial Intelligence):** The ability of machines to mimic human cognitive functions, such as learning and problem-solving.
- **Machine Learning (ML):** A subfield of AI that allows machines to learn and improve without explicit programming.
- **Deep Learning:** A type of machine learning inspired by the structure and function of the human brain, using artificial neural networks.
- **Large Language Models (LLMs):** AI systems trained on massive amounts of text data to communicate and generate human-like text in response to a wide range of prompts and questions.
- **ChatGPT:** An LLM developed by OpenAI, capable of generating different creative text formats, translating languages, writing different kinds of creative content, and answering your questions in an informative way. (Bonus Tip: Explore the capabilities of ChatGPT at https://chat.openai.com/)
- **Prompt Engineering:** The art of crafting clear and specific instructions that guide LLMs like ChatGPT towards generating the desired content or response.

This dictionary serves as a starting point for your exploration of the ever-expanding world of AI terminology. As you delve deeper into this field, you'll encounter even more exciting terms and concepts.

Knowledge is power. Equip yourself with the vocabulary and understanding necessary to navigate the world of AI with confidence and unleash your entrepreneurial potential.

www.ingramcontent.com/pod-product-compliance
Lightning Source LLC
Chambersburg PA
CBHW030051230526
45471CB00003B/1050